The Knowledge
book of
INSULTS

Edited by Jon Connell

Illustrations
by Maddy Fletcher

First published in 2024 by
Connell Publishing
Spye Arch House
Spye Park
Lacock
Wiltshire
SN15 2PR

10 9 8 7 6 5 4 3 2 1

Copyright © Connell Publishing Ltd.

All rights reserved. No part of this publication
may be reproduced, stored in a retrieval system or transmitted in any
form, or by any means (electronic, mechanical, or otherwise) without
the prior written permission of both the copyright owners
and the publisher.

A CIP catalogue record for this book is available from the British Library.
ISBN 978-1-911187-75-2

Printed in Great Britain

See our selection of literary and history guides at
www.connellguides.com

www.theknowledge.com

Contents

Introduction	4
Men & women	6
Marriage	24
The young	34
Professionals	42
Politicians	54
Britain & abroad	74
Writers	94
The way we live now	120

Introduction

"A gentleman is one who has too much good sense to be affronted by insults, is too well employed to remember insults, and too indolent to bear malice." So said the great Victorian clergyman, Cardinal Newman. But some insults, surely, deserve to be remembered. Let's face it: people are often at their most entertaining when they're insulting other people.

I have made no attempt here to be systematic or alphabetical; this is just a personal selection, and a short one, the guiding principle being very much that less is more. I have concentrated more on the present than the past, or at least the distant past: there's no Shakespeare here and not much from ancient times.

That said, I haven't worried much about who's doing the insulting or who's being insulted. In one issue of The Knowledge, when we quoted Jeremy Clarkson saying that Britain "is never so bad that Germany's better", we received a plaintive response from an Australian living in Germany. She was offended, she said, to see her "chosen country of residence" so traduced. We wrote back pointing out that in our quotes we had managed to insult most countries in Europe; we could hardly make an exception of Germany.

It's a reminder that, enjoyable as insults can be, we shouldn't take them too seriously. Waspish, imaginative, funny, they are often, like much good writing, the product of irritation or frustration or even anger. But then that's what makes them fun. "My aim," said the always entertaining playwright John Osborne, one of the so-called Angry Young Men, "is not to please, but to stimulate, not to flatter and lick but to needle and insult as cheerily as I can." Paul Johnson, the fiery right-wing author and commentator, once said that he used to read The Guardian to make himself cross before he wrote a column.

As with my book *Notes & Quotes* I've had invaluable help putting this collection together from my team at The Knowledge, in particular Michele Lavery, Harry Byford and Charlie Lyons. Thanks, too, to Iona Blayney, who runs Connell Guides, for so ably laying it all out, dealing with publication and helping with the editing. Thanks to my family for lots of shrewd advice and thanks, last but by no means least, to Maddy Fletcher for her wonderful drawings.

One final point: if eagle-eyed readers notice a little overlap with *Notes & Quotes* this is entirely deliberate: there are a few insults in *Notes & Quotes* which were simply too good to leave out of this volume.

Jon Connell, June 2024

MEN & WOMEN

"Brigands demand your money or your life; women require both."
Attrib. to Samuel Butler

"Being a woman is a terribly difficult trade since it consists principally of dealings with men."
Joseph Conrad

"Women are like elephants to me; they're nice to look at but I wouldn't want to own one."
WC Fields

"I wonder how girls manage to fall in love. It is easy to make them do it in books. But men are too ridiculous."
George Eliot

"If they can put one man on the moon, why not all of them?"
Feminist t-shirt

"I hate women because they always know where things are."
American humourist James Thurber

"Why are women so much more interesting to men than men are to women?"
Virginia Woolf

"A man who correctly guesses a woman's age may be smart, but he's not very bright."
American actress Lucille Ball

"The only place men want depth in a woman is in her cleavage."
Zsa Zsa Gabor

"Why did God create men? Because vibrators can't mow the lawn."
Madonna

"One of the few lessons
I have learned in life is
that there is invariably
something odd

about women who wear
ankle socks."
Alan Bennett

"She said she was approaching 40, and I couldn't help wondering from what direction."
**American comedian
Bob Hope**

"Give a man a free hand and he'll run it all over you."
Mae West

"When women gossip, we get called bitchy; but when men do it's called a podcast."
Comedian Sikisa Bostwick-Barnes

"It is only rarely that one can see in a little boy the promise of a man, but one can almost always see in a little girl the threat of a woman."
Alexandre Dumas

"Woman was God's second mistake."
Friedrich Nietzsche

"Men love with their eyes; women love with their ears."
Zsa Zsa Gabor

"Behind every great man is a woman rolling her eyes."
Jim Carrey

"The big difference between sex for money and sex for free is that sex for money usually costs a lot less."
Irish novelist and poet Brendan Behan

"That woman can speak 18 languages and she can't say 'no' in any of them."
Dorothy Parker of a guest surrounded by men at one of her parties

"What is the only thing that men and women have in common? I'll tell you. They both hate women."
Comedian Arabella Weir

Your concern for the rights of women
Is especially welcome news.
I'm sure you'll never exploit me;
I expect you'd rather be dead;
I'm thoroughly convinced of it –
Now can we go to bed?
Wendy Cope

"As the Prime Minister developed her case she, as it were, auto-fed her own indignation. It was a prototypical example of an argument with a woman – no rational sequence, associative, lateral thinking, jumping the rails the whole time."
Tory MP and diarist Alan Clark on Mrs Thatcher

"I am a marvellous housekeeper. Every time I leave a man, I keep his house."
Zsa Zsa Gabor

"A lasting relationship with a woman is possible only if you're a business failure."
J Paul Getty

"Well, it will make board meetings longer."
Unnamed American CEO when told his company had to have more women on its board

Settling Scores...

"There are probably more annoying things than being hectored about African developments by a wealthy Irish rock star in a cowboy hat, but I can't think of them at the moment."
Paul Theroux on Bono

You mention U2 in your article on the most annoying bands ever. The (possibly apocryphal) story goes that they were also subject to the greatest heckle ever. Halfway through a Dublin gig, Bono told the audience to hush and then started clicking his fingers. "Every time I click my fingers, somewhere a child dies," he said softly. Out of the gloom, a voice shouted out:
"Stop f***in' doing it, then."
Simon Miller of Thames Ditton in a letter to The Sunday Times

"Twin miracles of mascara, her eyes looked like the corpses of two small crows that had crashed into a chalk cliff."
Clive James on novelist Barbara Cartland

"[She] appeared to have put her lipstick on during an earth tremor."
Bill Bryson on an elderly guest in his hotel

"I always knew Frank would end up with a boy."
Ava Gardner on Frank Sinatra's marriage to Mia Farrow

"Miss Ferber you look almost like a man."
"And so do you Mr Coward."
Novelist Edna Ferber (wearing a tweed suit) and Noël Coward at the Algonquin Hotel in New York

"Sister Helen Loder was cycling through her parish when a boy shouted at her: 'F***** nun'. She dismounted from her bicycle and said: 'One or the other, but I can't be both.'"
Quoted by AN Wilson in the Evening Standard

"I think he honestly believes that it is churlish of us not to regard him as an exception, one who should be free of the network of obligation which binds everyone else."
Eton master Martin Hammond on Boris Johnson in a letter to Johnson's father in 1982

"I've polled 1,000 women asking if they would sleep with Boris. Twenty per cent said: 'Never again.'"
Pollster Frank Luntz, one of Johnson's contemporaries at Oxford

> "Take me or leave me; or, as is the usual order of things, both."
> **Dorothy Parker**

> "You must come again when you have less time."
> **Painter Walter Sickert to a departing guest**

> George the First was always reckoned
> Vile, but viler George the Second;
> And what mortal ever heard
> Any good of George the Third?
> When from Earth the Fourth descended
> (God be praised!) the Georges ended.
> **Walter Savage Landor**

"If all the girls who attended the Yale prom were laid end to end, I wouldn't be surprised."
Dorothy Parker

"The trouble with Ian is he gets off with women because he can't get on with them."
Novelist Rosamond Lehmann on Ian Fleming

"So boring you fell asleep halfway through her name."
Alan Bennett on writer Arianna Stassinopoulos

"I'd love to stop and chat but I'd rather have Type 2 diabetes."
Malcolm Tucker in *The Thick of It*

"Hang on, I'll just check my diary... Oh dear, I find I'm watching television that night."
Comedian Peter Cook when asked by David Frost to attend a dinner party with Prince Andrew

"When they circumcised Herbert Samuel, they threw away the wrong part."
David Lloyd George on his fellow Liberal politician

"A typical triumph of modern science to find the only part of Randolph that was not malignant and remove it."
Evelyn Waugh after Randolph Churchill had a lung (that turned out to be benign) removed.

"The man is so dense light bends around him."
Malcolm Tucker

"I once saved David Frost from drowning."
Peter Cook, asked if he had any regrets in life

"It's quite an achievement to be simultaneously the worst Corbyn and the worst Piers."
Michael Deacon on weather forecaster and conspiracy theorist Piers Corbyn in The Daily Telegraph

Famous Faces

"If Peter O'Toole was any prettier, they'd have to call it Florence of Arabia."
Noël Coward on O'Toole's TE Lawrence in *Lawrence of Arabia*

"I have a face that is a cross between two pounds of halibut and an explosion in an old clothes closet."
David Niven

"My face looks like a wedding cake left out in the rain."
WH Auden

"Eyes like rissoles in the snow."
Clive James on TV interviewer Michael Parkinson

"His ears make him look like a taxicab with both doors open."
Howard Hughes on Clark Gable

"I have a face like the behind of an elephant."
American actor Charles Laughton

Oh dearest Queen
I've never seen
A face more like
A soup-tureen
Anonymous on Elizabeth I

MARRIAGE

"I'm on a search for my future ex-wife."
American singer-songwriter Richie Sambora

"A man may be a fool and not know it, but not if he is married."
American journalist and critic HL Mencken

"I still miss my husband, but my aim is improving."
Old joke

"When a girl marries she exchanges the attention of many men for the inattention of one."
American journalist Helen Rowland

"There are two tragedies in life. One is to lose your heart's desire. The other is to gain it."
George Bernard Shaw

"Now at least I know where he is."
Queen Alexandra to Lord Esher after the death of her husband Edward VII, noted for his string of mistresses

"Never feel remorse for what you have thought about your wife; she has thought much worse things about you."
French biologist Jean Rostand

"I never married because there was no need. I have three pets at home which answer the same purpose as a husband. I have a dog that growls every morning, a parrot that swears all afternoon, and a cat that comes home late at night."
English novelist Marie Corelli

"Marriage is a long, dull meal with pudding as the first course."
Novelist JB Priestley

"Nothing is more distasteful than that entire complacency and satisfaction which beam in the countenance of a new-married couple."
English essayist Charles Lamb

"If you want to sacrifice the admiration of many men for the criticism of one, go ahead, get married."
American actress Katharine Hepburn

"The nearest some women get to being faithful to their husbands is being disagreeable to their lovers."
Novelist Anthony Powell

"The tragedy of marriage is that while all women marry thinking that their man will change, all men marry believing their wife will never change."
Novelist Len Deighton

"I bequeath all my property to my wife on condition that she remarry immediately. Then there will be at least one man to regret my death."
German poet Heinrich Heine

"It should be a very happy marriage – they are both so much in love with him."
Radio personality Irene Thomas

"Before you marry a person, you should first make them use a computer with slow internet to see who they really are."
American actor Will Ferrell

"I married beneath me – all women do."
**American-born British politician
Nancy Astor**

"A man doesn't know what happiness is until he marries. By then it's too late."
Frank Sinatra

"The best way to get most husbands to do something is to suggest that perhaps they're too old to do it."
American actress Anne Bancroft

"I haven't spoken to my mother-in-law in 18 months. I don't like to interrupt her."
Ken Dodd

"In Hollywood a marriage is a success if it outlasts milk."
American comedian Rita Rudner

"We love well only once, the first time. The loves which follow are less involuntary."
Jean de La Bruyère, 17th-century French philosopher

"They say the definition of ambivalence is watching your mother-in-law drive over a cliff in your new Cadillac."
Playwright David Mamet

"My first wife drove me to drink. It's the only thing I'm indebted to her for."
WC Fields

"Happiness is having a large, loving, caring, close-knit family in another city."
Comedian George Burns

"It was very good of God to let [Thomas] Carlyle and Mrs Carlyle marry one another and so make only two people miserable instead of four."
Samuel Butler

"Women may show some discrimination about whom they sleep with, but they'll marry anybody."
Anthony Powell

"Bigamy is having one wife too many. Monogamy is the same."
Oscar Wilde

"American women expect to find in their husbands a perfection that English women only hope to find in their butlers."
W Somerset Maugham

Advice from the Suffragettes

In 1911, the suffragettes issued their "advice on marriage to young ladies", says Shaun Usher in *Lists of Note*. Number one reads, quite simply: "Do not marry at all." "But if you must," it continues, avoid "the Beauty Men, Flirts... and the Football Enthusiasts". Even if you find a "Fire-lighter, Coal-getter, Window Cleaner and Yard Swiller", don't expect too much, for "most men are lazy, selfish, thoughtless, lying, drunken, clumsy, heavy-footed, rough, unmanly brutes". The advice continues: "If you want him to be happy, Feed the Brute. The same remark applies to Dogs."

THE YOUNG

"Blessed are the young, for they shall inherit the national debt."
Herbert Hoover, US president from 1929 to 1933

"If there's one thing I hate more than the Welsh it's the young. I hate young people with a passion. I wish them all ill. People under the age of 40 don't see anything. Even if they do, they don't really know what they are seeing."
TV dramatist Dennis Potter

"Parents – especially step-parents – are sometimes a bit of a disappointment to their children. They don't fulfil the promise of their early years."
Anthony Powell

"The first half of our lives is ruined by our parents, and the second half by our children."
American lawyer Clarence Darrow

"I love children, especially when they cry, for then someone takes them away."
Nancy Mitford

"The reasons grandparents and grandchildren get along so well is that they have a common enemy."
American humourist Sam Levenson

"Insanity is hereditary. You can get it from your children."
Ibid.

"Avenge yourself: live long enough to be a problem to one of your children."
Embroidery on one of Kirk Douglas's pillows

"A happy childhood has spoiled many a promising life."
Canadian author Robertson Davies

Etonians

"At Eton, you are trained not to talk about feelings, to be narrow-minded and to employ people who went to Winchester."
Film director Henry Cole

"He was educated at Eton and at Oxford, so Watson, bring the gun."
Sherlock Holmes

Changing times

"...all the stuff that made my generation proud to be British is now something to be ashamed of. The Spitfire caused global warming. Winston Churchill was a racist. The British Museum is full of stolen artefacts. The empire was wrong. Our famous comedy is misogynistic. Our stiff upper lip causes mental health issues. Kenny Everett was transphobic. Led Zeppelin were guilty of cultural appropriation. And we were only able to give the world penicillin and the internet and television because of slavery. Which we invented. And which we only dropped after pressure from Abraham Lincoln."
Jeremy Clarkson in The Sunday Times

"Hello, Granny," said Perdita guardedly, making no attempt to kiss her grandmother...
"How's your new school?"
"Horrific."
"And have you decided what you're going to do when you grow up?"
Perdita smiled. "I'm going to get divorced."
"I beg your pardon."
"I'm going to marry a mega-rich businessman, catch him cheating on me, and take him to the cleaners..."
From *Polo*, by Jilly Cooper

PROFESSIONALS

"If management consultants had drafted the Sermon on the Mount, there would be no Christians anywhere."
Historian Peter Hennessy

"The only difference between doctors and lawyers is that lawyers merely rob you, whereas doctors rob you and kill you, too."
Anton Chekhov

"The reason academic politics are so bitter is that so little is at stake."
Henry Kissinger

"A professor is one who talks in someone else's sleep."
WH Auden

"Without education, we are in a horrible and deadly danger of taking educated people seriously."
GK Chesterton

"Old professors never die. They just lose their faculties."
Stephen Fry

The Old Bailey judge who sentenced the Kray twins to life in 1969 later said they'd told the truth only twice in the whole trial, "once when Reggie called a barrister a 'fat slob', and once when Ronnie said the judge was biased".
The Spectator

"A lawyer is a person who writes a 10,000-word document and calls it a brief."
Franz Kafka

Doctors

"Anybody who goes to see a psychiatrist ought to have his head examined."
American film producer Samuel Goldwyn

God and the doctor we both adore
But only when in danger, not before;
The danger o'er, both are alike requited,
God is forgotten and the doctor slighted.
John Owen, 17th-century Welsh epigrammist

"I have had three doctors in the last 50 years. Each of them recommended I give up. But each of them has now died."
David Hockney on smoking

Butlers

Michael Kenneally, butler to the Sykes family of Sledmere in Yorkshire, was in the great tradition of eccentric English butlers. When Kenneally died in 1999, it was reported that he liked to let off steam by roaring "Let the buggers wait" as the bell in the dining room rang and rang, and once entered the dining room on a bicycle, cycling round the table with a stack of plates till he overbalanced and crashed to the floor.

~~~~~~

Another famous English butler, recalled by David McKie in The Guardian, was kept on by his mistress despite his love of the bottle. One night, however, when a well-known statesman came for dinner, he was so incapable that she wrote him a note. "You are drunk and disgusting," it said. "Please leave the room at once." The butler "surveyed it blearily, then shuffled uncertainly to the place where the statesman sat and plonked it down on his plate. "Her ladyship," he mumbled, "asked me to give you this."

Cricketers

"Would you like me to bowl you a piano and see if you can play that?"
Merv Hughes to Graham Gooch

Shane Warne: "I've been waiting two years for another chance to bowl at you."
Daryll Cullinan: "Looks like you spent it eating."

Actors

"You can pick out actors by the glazed look that comes into their eyes when the conversation wanders away from themselves."
English actor Michael Wilding

"Acting is the most minor of gifts and not a very high-class way to earn a living. Shirley Temple could do it at the age of four."
Katharine Hepburn

"She ran the gamut of human emotions all the way from A to B."
Dorothy Parker on Katharine Hepburn

"When I read about the lives of celebrities in our newspapers, I sometimes wish we had a Freedom From Information Act."
Theodore Dalrymple

"She was good at playing abstract confusion in the same way that a midget is good at being short."
Clive James on Marilyn Monroe

"Overweight, overbosomed, overpaid and under-talented, she set the acting profession back a decade."
David Susskind on Elizabeth Taylor in *Cleopatra*

"At 34 she is an extremely beautiful woman, lavishly endowed by nature with a few flaws in the masterpiece; she has an insipid double chin, her legs are too short, and she has a slight pot belly. She has a wonderful bosom, though."
Richard Burton on Elizabeth Taylor (who he married – twice)

"Playing Shakespeare is very tiring. You never get to sit down, unless you're a king."
American actress Josephine Hull

"Dear Ingrid – speaks five languages and can't act in any of them."
Sir John Gielgud on Ingrid Bergman

"The most meaningless legs imaginable."
British journalist Ivor Brown on John Gielgud

"I fail to see why not. Everyone else has."
Noël Coward on seeing a poster for Michael Redgrave and Dirk Bogarde in *The Sea Shall Not Have Them*

> "If you say 'Hiya, Clark, how are you?' he's stuck for an answer."
> **Ava Gardner on Clark Gable**

> "You can count on Errol Flynn. He'll always let you down."
> **David Niven**

Faye Dunaway: "What's my motivation in this scene?"
Roman Polanski: "Your salary."
Exchange on the set of *Chinatown*

POLITICIANS

"Vote for Guy Fawkes. The only man to enter parliament with honest intent."
Spotted on a poster during the 1979 general election

"A gaffe is the opposite of a lie: it is when a politician inadvertently tells the truth."
Michael Kinsley

"I don't make jokes. I just watch the government and report the facts."
American humourist Will Rogers

"Democracy is the process by which people choose who to blame."
Philosopher Bertrand Russell

"A chilling characteristic of politicians is that they're not in it for the money."
HL Mencken

"He has not a single redeeming defect."
Benjamin Disraeli on William Gladstone

"You can fool too many people too much of the time."
James Thurber

"True terror is to wake up one morning and realise that your high school class is running the country."
American novelist Kurt Vonnegut

"Politics is supposed to be the second-oldest profession. I have come to realise that it bears a very close resemblance to the first."
Ronald Reagan

"How can they tell?"
Dorothy Parker on being told that former US president Calvin Coolidge was dead

"The difference between a misfortune and a calamity is this: If Gladstone fell into the Thames, it would be a misfortune. But if someone dragged him out again, that would be a calamity."
Disraeli on Gladstone

"He has all of the virtues I dislike, and none of the vices I admire."
Winston Churchill on one of his opponents

Lord Sandwich: "Wilkes, I don't know whether you will die of the pox or on the gallows."
Wilkes: "That depends on whether I embrace your lordship's mistress or his principles."

"[Sir Robert] Peel's smile was like the silver plate on a coffin."
Irish Nationalist leader and MP Daniel O'Connell

"You can fool some of the people all of the time, and those are the ones you need to concentrate on."
Advice by American political activist Robert Strauss to George W Bush

"He's so dumb he couldn't tip shit out of a boot if the instructions were written on the heel."
Lyndon Johnson on Gerald Ford

Nancy Astor: "Winston, if you were my husband, I'd poison your tea."
Churchill: "Nancy, if I were your husband, I'd drink it."

"He occasionally stumbled over the truth, but hastily picked himself up and hurried on as if nothing had happened."
Churchill on Anthony Eden

"Winston, you are drunk."
"You're right, Bessie. And you are ugly. But tomorrow morning I'll be sober."
Churchill to Bessie Braddock

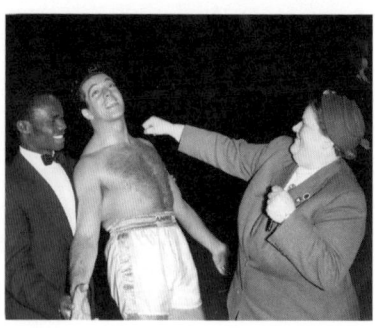

"A modest man with much to be modest about."
Churchill on Clement Attlee

"An empty cab drew up outside Parliament and Clement Attlee got out."
Ibid.

"A man who plays the bagpipes in his spare time is obviously not a friend to humanity."
Julie Burchill on Alastair Campbell

"The nine most terrifying words in the English language are 'I'm from the government and I'm here to help'."
Ronald Reagan

"The government consists of a gang of men exactly like you and me. They have, taken one with another, no special talent for the business of government; they have only a talent for getting and holding office."
HL Mencken

"Remember, democracy never lasts long. It soon wastes, exhausts and murders itself. There never was a democracy yet that did not commit suicide."
**John Adams, US president
1797 to 1801**

"He told us he was going to take crime out of the streets. He did. He took it into the damn White House."
The Reverend Ralph Abernathy on Richard Nixon

"In a disastrous fire in President Reagan's library both books were destroyed. And the real tragedy is that he hadn't finished colouring one."
American lawyer and politician Jonathan Hunt

"The most dangerous duo, President Ray-Gun and the plutonium blonde, Margaret Thatcher."
Union leader Arthur Scargill

"She sounded like the Book of Revelation read out over a railway public address system by a headmistress of a certain age wearing calico knickers."
Clive James on Margaret Thatcher

"Great supine protoplasmic invertebrate jellies."
Boris Johnson on the London Assembly

Those who rule us...

They have given us into the hands
Of the new unhappy lords:
Lords without anger or honour
Who dare not carry their swords.
They fight by shuffling papers,
They have bright dead alien eyes
And they look on our labour and laughter
As a tired man watches flies.
The load of their loveless pity
Is worse than the ancient wrongs:
Their doors are shut in the evening
And they know no songs.

We hear men speaking for us of new laws strong and sweet,
Yet is there no man speaketh as we speak in the street.
It may be we shall rise the last as Frenchmen rose the first,
Our wrath come after Russia's wrath and our wrath be the worst.
It may be we are meant to mark with our riot and our rest
God's scorn for all men governing. It may be beer is best.

But we are the people of England; and we have not spoken yet.
Smile at us, pay us, pass us. But do not quite forget.

From *The Secret People,* GK Chesterton

~~~~~~

It's all in the name

"I'm a great believer in nominative determinism," wrote Matthew Parris in The Times in early 2023, which doesn't bode well for our current crop of MPs. Given the trouble we had with Chris Pincher, it's alarming that a fellow called Greg Hands has been appointed Tory party chairman. There are "two Bacons rootling around in the Westminster undergrowth", and a Blunt "not always noted for his tact". "I know of no association between Cash and brown envelopes, but 'Hazzard for prime minister' would worry the nation, Skidmore sounds unsteady and, as for Rimmer, let's not go there." It all adds to my theory that today's MPs are often yesterday's kids who were teased in the playground. "The angels weep for a boy called Hancock."

Presidents and prime ministers

In the run-up to the 1997 general election, John Major visited the former Sun editor Kelvin MacKenzie at his office in a Canary Wharf skyscraper. Looking out of the window, the prime minister commented: "Incredible view you've got from here, Kelvin." "Yes," replied MacKenzie. "On a clear day, you can almost see a Tory voter."
Mark Mason in The Spectator

When Queen Elizabeth held a dinner in 1985 for her six surviving prime ministers, James Callaghan asked if anyone knew the collective noun for former PMs. Harold Macmillan had the best answer: "A lack of principals."

On the day Lyndon Johnson was sworn in as vice president in 1961, the former congresswoman Clare Boothe Luce asked him why he had given up a powerful position in the Senate for his relatively powerless new office. "Clare," he replied, "I looked it up. One out of every four presidents has died in office. I'm a gamblin' man, darlin', and this is the only chance I got." Two years later, President Kennedy was assassinated and LBJ took over.

~~~~~~~~

When a woman told President Calvin Coolidge at a party that she'd taken a bet that she could conjure at least three words out of him, he replied: "You lose."
Quoted by David McKie in The Guardian

"It would have been splendid... if the wine had been as cold as the soup, the beef as rare as the service, the brandy as old as the fish, and the maid as willing as the duchess."
Churchill on a dinner

And so while the great ones depart to their dinner,
the secretary stays, getting thinner and thinner,
racking his brains to record and report
what he thinks that they think
they ought to have thought.
Historian Arthur Bryant

"When I came to the Treasury, they predicted to me that I would become the most unpopular man in Britain. This was the only correct forecast the Treasury made in the several years I was chancellor."
Norman Lamont

"God help the Tory party if the Tories ever get hold of it."
Matthew Parris

"The urge to pass new laws must be seen as an illness, not much different from the urge to bite old women."
Journalist Auberon Waugh

Liberals

"We who are liberal and progressive know that the poor are our equal in every sense except that of being equal to us."
American literary critic Lionel Trilling

"Powerful imaginations are conservative."
Austrian novelist Hugo von Hofmannsthal

"Very often the most intolerant and narrow-minded people are the ones who congratulate themselves on their tolerance and open-mindedness."
Christopher Hitchens

"That dreary tribe of high-minded women and sandal-wearers and bearded fruit-juice drinkers who come flocking towards the smell of 'progress' like bluebottles to a dead cat."
George Orwell

"A liberal is a man too broad-minded to take his own side in a quarrel."
American poet Robert Frost

"A liberal is just a conservative who hasn't been mugged."
South African self-defence expert Hilton Hamann

"Liberals have invented whole college majors – psychology, sociology, women's studies – to prove that nothing is anybody's fault."
PJ O'Rourke

"At the core of liberalism is the spoilt child – miserable, as all spoilt children are, unsatisfied, demanding, ill-disciplined, despotic and useless. Liberalism is a philosophy of snivelling brats."
Ibid.

"A liberal is a conservative who's been arrested."
American writer Tom Wolfe

"I was raised a socialist. I'm trying to earn enough to become a socialist again."
Comedian Shaparak Khorsandi

A conservative is one "who is enamoured of existing evils, as distinguished from the Liberal who wishes to replace them with others".
Ambrose Bierce

"Inside every revolutionary there is a policeman."
Gustave Flaubert

BRITAIN & ABROAD

"The English are not a very spiritual people, so they invented cricket to give them some idea of eternity."

George Bernard Shaw

"England is perhaps the only great country whose intellectuals are ashamed of their own nationality."
George Orwell

"England is not a bad country – it's just a mean, cold, ugly, divided, clapped-out, post-imperial, post-industrial slag heap covered in polystyrene hamburger cartons."
Novelist Margaret Drabble

"A soggy little island huffing and puffing to keep up with Western Europe."
American novelist John Updike

"When an Englishman gets run down by a truck he apologises to the truck."
American comedian Jackie Mason

"Mean, envious, full of rancour, hatred and self-righteousness."
Auberon Waugh on the British

"My mother had a theory about Englishmen: They are permanently all two gin and tonics under par. They need two gin and tonics to become human."
Hugh Grant

"In six short weeks Britain has acquired Italian-style politics and finances, without the sunshine."
Journalist Camilla Cavendish in 2022

"This English woman is so refined
She has no bosom and no behind."
Poet and novelist Stevie Smith

Wales

"The Earth contains no race of human beings so totally vile and worthless as the Welsh."
**Writer and poet
Walter Savage Landor**

"The relationship between the Welsh and the English is based on trust and understanding. They don't trust us and we don't understand them."
**Rugby union player and official
Dudley Wood**

"The land of my fathers. My fathers can have it."
Dylan Thomas on Wales

Scotland

"The Scotchman is one who keeps the Sabbath and everything else he can lay his hands on."
Lyndon Johnson

"There are two seasons in Scotland: June and winter."
Billy Connolly

"It is never difficult to distinguish between a Scotsman with a grievance and a ray of sunshine."
PG Wodehouse

Ireland

"The Irish are a very fair people – they never speak well of one another."
Dr Johnson

"Because a man is born in a stable, that doesn't make him a horse."
The Duke of Wellington denying he was Irish

Europe

"Heaven in Europe: the English are the policemen, the French the cooks, the Germans the mechanics, the Italians the lovers, and the Swiss organise everything. Hell in Europe: the Germans are the policemen, the English the cooks, the French the mechanics, the Swiss the lovers, and the Italians organise everything."
Old EU gag quoted by Judith Woods in The Daily Telegraph

"Europe was set up by clever, Catholic, left-wing, French bureaucrats. Most Brits have a problem with at least three of those five."
Peter Hennessy

Italy

"I take care to only travel on Italian ships. In the event of disaster, there is none of that nonsense about women and children first."
Noël Coward

"I saw the new Italian navy. Its boats have glass bottoms so they can see the old Italian navy."
Peter Secchia, President Bush's nominee for US Ambassador to Italy, during Senate confirmation hearings, 1989

Germany

"Life is never so bad that Germany is better."
Jeremy Clarkson

"German humour is no laughing matter."
Mark Twain

"A German wine label is one of the things life's too short for."
Kingsley Amis

"I like Germany so much, I think there should be two of them."
French novelist François Mauriac on German reunification

Switzerland

"In Italy for 30 years under the Borgias they had warfare, terror, murder, bloodshed – they produced Michelangelo, Leonardo da Vinci and the Renaissance.

In Switzerland they had brotherly love, 500 years of democracy and peace, and what did they produce? The cuckoo clock."

Orson Welles in *The Third Man*

France

"When God created France He found it so perfect that, to comfort those who couldn't live there, He invented the French."
Old saying

"We always have been, we are, and I hope that we always shall be detested in France."
The Duke of Wellington

Africa

"Democracy in Africa means one man, one vote, once."
Ian Smith, former prime minister of Rhodesia (now Zimbabwe)

America

"What a pity, when Christopher Columbus discovered America, that he ever mentioned it."
Margot Asquith

"It is absurd to say that there are neither ruins nor curiosities in America when they have their mothers and their manners."
Oscar Wilde

"America is just a big version of [the] Westfield [shopping centre] but with witty people round the edges and a desert in the middle."
Journalist Kevin Maher

"If you're thinking of coming to America, this is what it's like: you've got your Comfort Inn, you've got your Best Western, and you've got your Red Lobster where you eat. Everybody's very fat, everybody's very stupid and everybody's very rude – it's not a holiday programme, it's the truth."
Jeremy Clarkson

"Wherever there's injustice, oppression and suffering, America will show up six months late and bomb the country next to where it's happening."
PJ O'Rourke

"On some great and glorious day, the plain folks of the land will reach their heart's desire at last, and the White House will be adorned with a moron."
HL Mencken

"They're rich and we're poor.
But we're smart and they're dumb.
So we'd better tell them what to do."
**Old Whitehall saying about the
British view of America**

"You will find the Americans much as
the Greeks found the Romans: great,
big, vulgar, bustling people more
vigorous than we are and also more
idle, with more unspoiled virtues but
also more corrupt."
Harold Macmillan on Americans

"California is a place where they
shoot too many pictures and not
enough actors."
**American journalist
Walter Winchel**

"Most of American life is driving somewhere and then driving back wondering why the hell you went."
John Updike

"I come from Des Moines, Iowa. Somebody had to."
Bill Bryson's opening line of his first book

"The difference between yoghurt and Los Angeles is that yoghurt has a living culture."
Sean Penn

To the comment "You'll have the vote of every thinking American", **Adlai Stevenson** replied: 'That's not enough, I need a majority."

"To be America's enemy may be dangerous, but to be its friend is fatal."
Henry Kissinger

"Be nice to America – or we'll bring you democracy."
US bumper sticker after the invasion of Iraq

"American society is pyramid-shaped. The further down you go, the wider people grow."
Craig Brown

"The men the American people admire most extravagantly are the most daring liars; the men they detest most violently are those who try to tell them the truth."
HL Mencken

"The explanation is quite simple. I wished to be near my mother."
Artist James Whistler when asked why he'd been born in such an unfashionable place as Lowell, Massachusetts

Australia

"It raises the average IQ of both countries."
Robert Muldoon, former prime minister of New Zealand, on the exodus of New Zealanders emigrating to Australia

"To live in Australia permanently is rather like going to a party and dancing all night with one's mother."
Barry Humphries

Russia

> "Every country has its own mafia. Putin's Russia is the first where the mafia has its own country."
> **Garry Kasparov**

Mikhail Gorbachev had a good sense of humour, says the columnist **George Will**. When the Soviet leader arrived late for an event at the Kremlin because he'd been dealing with a problem in the agricultural sector, a French official asked when the issue had arisen. "In 1917," he replied.

WRITERS

"If you can't annoy somebody with what you write, I think there's little point in writing."
Kingsley Amis

> "Some editors are failed writers, but so are most writers."
> **TS Eliot**

> "William Douglas Home, pronounced Hume, who makes me foam, pronounced fume."
> **Kenneth Tynan on the Scottish playwright**

> "If I had to live my life all over again, I'd do it exactly the same – only I wouldn't read *Beowulf*."
> **Woody Allen**

> "Me no Leica."
> **Theatre critic Kenneth Tynan reviewing the show *I Am a Camera***

"What? Do you mean the damn sewer invented it?"
Lord Redesdale, on being told Hardy's *Tess of the d'Urbervilles* was not a true story

"It is a shame [Jane Austen] died peacefully. Every time I read *Pride and Prejudice* I want to dig her up and beat her over the skull with her own shin-bone."*
Mark Twain

"A hack writer who would not have been considered fourth rate in Europe, who tricked out a few of the old proven 'surefire' literary skeletons with sufficient local colour to intrigue the superficial and the lazy."
William Faulkner on Mark Twain

---

* The "every time" is interesting. It's odd to keep rereading a book you dislike so much.

"From the moment I picked up your book until I laid it down I was convulsed with laughter. Some day I intend reading it."
Groucho Marx on American humourist SJ Perelman

"In my twenties the critics said I was brutal, in my thirties they said I was flippant, in my forties they said I was cynical, in my fifties they said I was competent, and now in my sixties they say I am superficial. I have gone my way, following the course I had mapped out for myself."
W Somerset Maugham in *The Summing Up*

"Those compendiums of other journalists' mistakes which newspapers laughably call libraries."
Evelyn Waugh

"I became a journalist partly so that I wouldn't ever have to rely on the press for my information."
Christopher Hitchens

"The covers of this book are too far apart."
Ambrose Bierce in a review

"If I see 'upcoming' in the paper one more time, I will be downcoming and someone will be outgoing."
Former managing editor of The Wall Street Journal Barney Kilgore

"My God, what a clumsy *olla putrida* James Joyce is! Nothing but old fags and cabbage stumps of quotations from the Bible and the rest stewed in the juice of deliberate, journalistic dirty-mindedness."
DH Lawrence

"An essentially private man who wanted his total indifference to public notice to be universally recognised."
Tom Stoppard on Joyce

"To watch him fumbling with our rich and delicate English language is like seeing a Sèvres vase in the hands of a chimpanzee."
Evelyn Waugh on the poet Stephen Spender

"Once again, words fail Norman Mailer."
Gore Vidal after being punched by Mailer in a fit of rage

"I have been bitten, I must avoid infection/Or else I'll be as dead as Naipaul's fiction."
Saint Lucian poet Derek Walcott on VS Naipaul

"He doesn't know what he means and he doesn't know he doesn't know."
Literary critic FR Leavis on novelist CP Snow

Private Eye

"...like his three heroes, [Richard Ingrams] is a reactionary, in the sense that he is sure only of what he is against. He and the [Private] Eye crew forgive nothing to anyone else and everything to themselves. So it is that Ingrams is able on the one hand to write a book as sensitive as this, and on the other to let one of Private Eye's anonymous gossip columnists fulfil a lifetime's ambition, which is to tell dirty stories about the people he envies, and send their children crying home from school.
Clive James on Richard Ingrams, former editor of Private Eye, reviewing *God's Apostles*

The Guardian

"Must we really shatter the tranquillity of this charmingly eccentric and ultimately harmless London institution, purely in the name of social engineering?" Why shouldn't the high-born have a newspaper of their own? These "specious arguments" will be trotted out by commentators determined to maintain the status quo – to ensure that all the paper's thinkpieces about poverty and capitalist greed "continue to be written by people who went on school trips to Val d'Isère". But we must not give up. We will never achieve true equality in Britain until "this ancient bastion of privilege is finally dragged kicking and screaming into the modern world".
The Daily Telegraph's Michael Deacon on his "campaign" to persuade The Guardian to hire state-educated journalists

"A critic is a man who knows the way but can't drive the car."
Kenneth Tynan

"There is bad in all good authors; what a pity the converse isn't true."
Philip Larkin

"Every journalist has a novel inside him, which is an excellent place for it."
Russell Lynes (a journalist)

"I didn't like the play, but then I saw it under adverse conditions – the curtain was up."
Groucho Marx

"Perhaps the whole odd shape of American fiction arises simply (as simplifying Europeans are always quick to assure us) because there is no real sexuality in American life and therefore cannot very well be any in American art. What we cannot achieve in our relations with each other it would be vain to ask our writers to portray..."
American literary critic Leslie Fiedler in *Love and Death in the American Novel*, **1960**

"With some exceptions in science fiction and other genres I have small difficulty in avoiding anything that could be called American literature. I feel it is unnatural, not I think entirely because it uses a language that is not mine, however closely akin to my own."
Kingsley Amis in *The King's English: A Guide to Modern Usage*

"George Bernard Shaw, most poisonous of all the poisonous haters of England; despiser, distorter, and denier of the plain truths by which men live… irresponsible braggart, blaring self-trumpeter, idol of opaque intellectuals and thwarted females…"
English dramatist Henry Jones

"Concerning no subject would Shaw be deterred by the minor accident of total ignorance from penning a definitive opinion."
Roger Scruton

"I'm all for the freedom of the press. It's the newspapers I can't stand."
Tom Stoppard in *Night and Day*

"He has never been known to use a word that might send a reader to the dictionary."
William Faulkner on Ernest Hemingway

"Does he really think big emotions come from big words?"
Hemingway on Faulkner

"I have only ever read one book in my life, and that was *White Fang*. It was so good I've never bothered to read another."
Uncle Matthew in Nancy Mitford's *Love in a Cold Climate*

"The difference between fiction and reality? Fiction has to make sense."
American novelist Tom Clancy

"Novels today are all about women being sad in Fulham."
Kingsley Amis

"The book was originally to be called Who Cares, and perhaps that title should have been retained."
Ann Manov on Lauren Oyler's essay collection, *No Judgement*

"He could not blow his nose without moralising about conditions in the handkerchief industry."
Cyril Connolly on George Orwell

"Oh really. What is she reading?"
Actress Edith Evans to a friend who said Nancy Mitford was borrowing her villa to finish a book

"It's his 19th book... Here's hoping it's his last."
Steve Donoghue on Henry Kissinger's *Leadership: Six Studies in World Strategy*

The trials of authorship

One of the books edited by the veteran New York editor Robert Gottlieb was Bill Clinton's 2004 autobiography. "This is the single most boring page I have ever read," he wrote at one point in the manuscript. The former president wrote his own note beside it: "No. Page 632 is even more boring."
The Washington Post

"When the former Lib Dem leader Paddy Ashdown gave me a copy of his book, I was disappointed to see there was no inscription in the front. But when I turned to my own name in the index, I found a specially written message: 'I thought you'd look here first, love Paddy.'"
Rory Stewart on The Rest is Politics

At his home in Hertfordshire, **George Bernard Shaw** had a writing shed that he called "London". The idea was that unwanted visitors could be honestly told by staff that he was "in London".

At a mutual friend's birthday, I once found myself seated with the Queen, says **Charles Moore** in The Spectator. "Philip," she said, "is reading your book and enjoying it very much. But I gather there's more to come." "Yes, ma'am," I replied, "I'm frightfully sorry, but I'm afraid there will be a third volume." "Oh, don't worry," said the Queen, "I shan't read it!" I felt proud to be in the same situation as Edward Gibbon presenting his latest volume of *The Decline and Fall of the Roman Empire* to King George III's brother, the Duke of Gloucester. "Another damn'd thick, square book!" said the Duke. "Always, scribble, scribble, scribble, eh, Mr Gibbon."

"Rupert Grint has said that he likens 'JK Rowling to an auntie — I don't necessarily agree with everything my auntie says, but she's still my auntie'. It's so sweet. I am sure next time I hang my own auntie out to dry at the hands of a baying hate mob for callous reasons of professional opportunism and deep moral cowardice, I will think of Rupert Grint, and smile. Like a wolf."
Giles Coren in The Times

Art & music

"Skill without imagination is craftmanship and gives us many useful objects such as wickerwork picnic baskets. Imagination without skill gives us modern art."
Tom Stoppard

"Art today is institutionalised narcissism, a conspiracy between creators and curators to make poor people feel stupid."
**Welsh writer and critic
Stephen Bayley**

"The masses' bad taste is more deeply rooted in reality than the intellectuals' good taste."
Bertolt Brecht

"Perhaps not, but then you can't call yourself a great work of nature."
James Whistler, after a sitter complained that his portrait was not a great work of art

"Jazz is the only form of music that the musicians seem to be enjoying more than the audience."
Anonymous

"Liam is the angriest man you'll ever meet. He's like a man with a fork in a world of soup."
Noel Gallagher on his brother

"Those who have never heard it for themselves may recreate it in the comfort and privacy of their own homes by setting fire to the tail of their pet cat."
Craig Brown on Yoko Ono's song, *Don't Worry Kyoko (Mummy's Only Putting Her Hand in the Snow)*

"If a horse could sing in a monotone, the horse would sound like Carly Simon, only a horse wouldn't rhyme 'yacht', 'apricot', and 'gavotte'."
American critic Robert Christgau

"Far too noisy, my dear Mozart. Far too many notes."
Archduke Ferdinand on *The Marriage of Figaro*

"Wagner has beautiful moments, but awful quarters of an hour."
Italian composer Gioachino Rossini

"Wagner's music is better than it sounds."
Mark Twain

"Mick Jagger has big lips. I saw him suck an egg out of a chicken. He can play a tuba from both ends. This man has got childbearing lips."
Joan Rivers

"Well, not bad, but there are decidedly too many of them, and they are not very well arranged. I would have done it differently."
James Whistler, when asked if he thought the stars were especially beautiful one night

"She's so pure Moses couldn't part her knees."
Joan Rivers on singer Marie Osmond

"He has Van Gogh's ear for music."
Austrian-born film director Billy Wilder

"Classic FM: for people who like classical music, but only if it's been on an advert."
Comedy character Alan Partridge (played by Steve Coogan)

Fan: "You don't know who I am, but I know who you are."
Bob Dylan: "Let's keep it that way."

THE WAY WE LIVE NOW

"The only people we think of as normal are those we don't know very well."
Sigmund Freud

"Never trust people who smile constantly. They're either selling something or not very bright."
American writer Laurell Hamilton

"Always look for the fool in the deal. If you don't find one, it's you."
American entrepreneur Mark Cuban

"This man is depriving a village somewhere of an idiot."
Extract from Royal Navy and Marines fitness report, 1997

"Those who can, do. Those who can't, teach. Those who can't teach, teach gym."
Woody Allen

"Weak people never give way when they ought to."
French churchman Cardinal de Retz

"Many people would sooner die than think. In fact, they do."
Bertrand Russell

"It's always tempting to impute/ Unlikely virtues to the cute."
PJ O'Rourke

"A common mistake that people make when trying to design something completely foolproof is to underestimate the ingenuity of complete fools."
Author Douglas Adams

"The power of accurate observation is generally called cynicism by those who have not got it."
George Bernard Shaw

"Anyone going slower than you is an idiot and anyone going faster than you is a maniac."
Comedian Jerry Seinfeld on drivers

"Don't forgive and never forget; do unto others before they do unto you; and third and most importantly, keep your eye on your friends, because your enemies will take care of themselves."
Larry Hagman as JR in *Dallas*

"Only the shallow know themselves."
Oscar Wilde

"Great minds tend towards banality."
French author André Gide

"Think of how stupid the average person is, and realise half of them are stupider than that."
American critic and comedian George Carlin

"Fundamentalists lack that most civilising of human virtues: doubt."
Journalist Matthew Syed

"Some ideas are so preposterous that only an intellectual could believe them."
George Orwell

"How fond men are of justice when it comes to judging the crimes of former generations."
French dramatist Armand Salacrou

"I do not believe that friends are necessarily the people you like best, they are merely the people who got there first."
Peter Ustinov

"There is no sunrise so beautiful that it's worth waking me up to see it."

American comedian Mindy Kaling

"One of the delights known to age, and beyond the grasp of youth, is that of Not Going."
JB Priestley

"He was gifted with the sly, sharp instinct for self-preservation that passes for wisdom among the rich."
Evelyn Waugh in *Scoop*

"Wall Street indices predicted nine out of the last five recessions."
American economist Paul Samuelson

"Ok. We can walk to the kerb from here."
Woody Allen to Diane Keaton after she parks her car in *Annie Hall*

> "There are blundering armies of nosy and interfering 'caring' maniacs. Their compassionate masks conceal a vindictive, retributive energy."
> **Playwright John Osborne in 1992**

Fame

Thomas Carney, the crusty scouse bartender at Manhattan's famous Elaine's saloon, had no time for self-important customers. According to his obituary in The New York Times, when a big-shot guest started arguing over his bill, demanding "Do you know who I am?" Carney climbed on top of the bar, "clanged a spoon on a bottle", and announced: "This man does not know who he is. Does anybody know who he is? We need help."

Christmas

"What an awful time of year this is! Just as one is feeling that if one can just hold on, it won't get any worse, then all this Christmas idiocy bursts upon one like a slavering Niagara of nonsense and completely wrecks one's entire frame. This means, in terms of my life, making a point of buying about six simple inexpensive presents when there are rather more people about than usual, and going home. No doubt in terms of yours it means seeing your house given over to hoards of mannerless middle-class brats and your good food and drink vanishing into the quacking tooth-equipped jaws of their alleged parents. Yours is the harder course, I can see. On the other hand, mine is happening to me."

Philip Larkin, in a letter to art historian Judy Egerton in 1958

Money

"When somebody says it's not about the money, it's about the money."
HL Mencken

"There are three kinds of economists. Those who can add, and those who can't."
Journalist Hamish McRae

"A woman whose husband has just died rings the Jewish Chronicle to put in an obituary notice. 'I just want to say: Harry Solomons has passed away,' she says. 'But our minimum payment is £20,' replies the woman at the Chronicle, 'so you're allowed up to three more words at no extra cost.' 'Ok,' says Mrs Solomons, 'you can add: Volvo for sale.'"
Michael Grade's favourite Jewish joke

"Man was made at the end of the week's work, when God was tired."
Mark Twain

"If other people are going to talk, conversation becomes impossible."
James Whistler

"We must believe in luck, for how else can we explain the success of those we don't like?"
French poet Jean Cocteau

"I sometimes think that God, in creating man, somewhat overestimated his ability."
Oscar Wilde

"There is no such thing as conversation. There are intersecting monologues, that's all."
British author Rebecca West

"Life is one long process of getting tired."
Samuel Butler

"Life is first boredom, then fear."
Philip Larkin

"Ah, scrambled eggs and bacon – the only two things in the world that never let you down."
Ian Fleming

"Only two things are infinite, the universe and human stupidity, and I'm not sure about the former."
Albert Einstein

The Knowledge is a free daily email with over 140,000 subscribers. Every day, we scour hundreds of newspapers, websites, and social media outlets, and pick out only the very best bits. Best of all, the whole thing takes just five minutes to read.

As we like to say, read less, know more.

To sign up, head to

www.theknowledge.com

To buy a copy of

The Knowledge Notes & Quotes

head to **www.theknowledgenotesandquotes.com**